T0145783

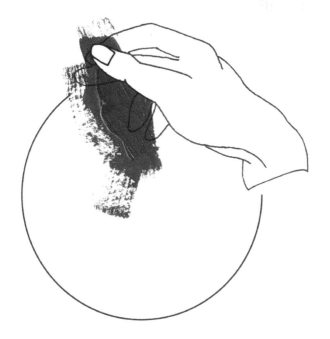

NOT A CULT

Los Angeles, CA
*notacult.media*

Printed in the USA

Bodney, Edwin
2nd edition.

ISBN: 978-1-945649-01-1

Edited by
Cover design by Cassidy Trier
Editorial design by Ian DeLucca

NOT A CULT
Los Angeles, CA

Printed in the United States of America

# Contents

because their language is hard

# LEFT HAND

## —Viewed from the back DORSAL SURFACE -

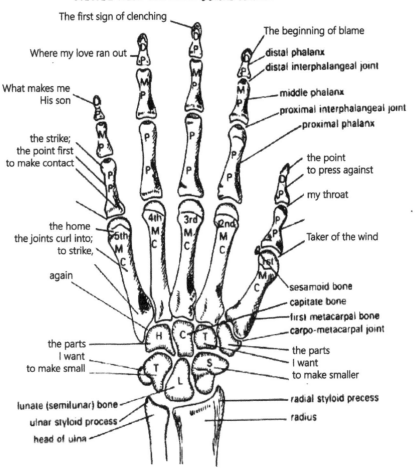

The first sign of clenching

The beginning of blame

Where my love ran out

distal phalanx

distal interphalangeal joint

What makes me
His son

middle phalanx

proximal interphalangeal joint

proximal phalanx

the strike;
the point first
to make contact

the point
to press against

my throat

the home
the joints curl into;
to strike,

Taker of the wind

again

sesamoid bone

capitate bone

first metacarpal bone

carpo-metacarpal joint

the parts
I want
to make small

the parts
I want
to make smaller

lunate (semilunar) bone

radial styloid precess

ulnar styloid process

radius

head of ulna

I pick apart many small thing: thread from a sweater we once owned, my fingernails, the skin on the tips of my thumbs; I can't read my prints anymore, but every veil is thinly broken/open to find the moment I thought I knew the man you were.

My father never asks about you—where you are, what you did, how many times. Even after all my blood has run itself into a manuscript he has read (more than once by now, I'm sure); does he see the hem unraveling—the place I am missing from, the place the rest used to hang?

# a study of hands

Hands have always been fascinating objects to me. They are
the first things I look at when I encounter a man. They say a lot
[the pit of the palm, if the knuckles laugh when the fist is made]
about a man's intimacy.      I've never liked my own hands; my
love is good though. I didn't always believe that. I was a tree-
child the first time I noticed my hands—always more legs than
anything.      Legs are running things.      The first time
a pair of hands made me smile into a question, my grandmother
crocheted, nestled into the corner of her old couch that collected
more dust than memories. I didn't look at tv no more.      The
first time they made me angry, I saw my father's hands wrapped
around *his* woman's arms.      He shook her into the same quiet
you hear the last time you walk into a home you have just
moved out of. She was mean, but I knew nobody deserved to be
touched like that.      The first time a pair woke me into a night
terror, he would not stop pulling me closer.      The second
time—

—mine is still good though.

# 2/30

Your body
A brown river

I am a smooth stone

Made light
And
Dirty in my skip

Made clean
And heavy
In your run

# a body, pt. 3

The skin is the body's first line of defense

How quickly
it
will throw
itself
between
You
and
The one who will take you;

Many months will pass, and
it will not give anything.

It will harden —
a forgotten,
stone slab
waiting to be trampled

It will constrict —
retract —
curdle even!

When someone asks for your permission

How the skin will defend,
and just as soon be the first thing to give you away

Like a father, on something like a wedding day.

# (when i begin to ask)

Who made you a stone,
Left you on the side of some dirty road?
Who has time to pick up stones these days?
How much space you got in those pockets?
Do you know how many stones you got hangin' inside those
pockets?
Are you a stone in your own pocket?

How will you get out?
How do you move when you don't move unless somebody moves
you?
Do you need somebody to move you?
Is it a body?
Is it someone else's body?
Do you have a body?
Is it only a stone now?
Can you be a body again?
Will you be somebody?
You sure you want to be a body again?
Does a body mean you are somebody?

Do you remember what you love?
Are you one of those things you remember?
What of the trees?
What of your grandmother's perfume?
Remember how simple it all was?
Do you remember her?
Do you know she gave birth to your father?
but this ain't about your father.

Have you moved yourself yet?

Are you still a stone now?

Have you become the one who hurt you?

# drift, boy

My grandmothers are the two women I love the most.

The first: Granny. My father's mother. Short. Fat. Black—almost
the texture of velvet. Her skin grinned before she did. She
raised six children with my grandfather's fist in her back, but she
tells me that it was okay because she didn't ask god for a second
marriage to a man who would not beat her, she only asked for a
man to provide for her children. He did that.
When granny's children got older, she'd say,
> *If I could have skipped y'all to get to your children, instead, I
> would have.*

{{Now, I don't think about what her children must've done to
make her say that, but I love knowing I'm the flock that came
after.}}

Granny drank her coffee black, fried chicken every day for the
ten of us; she made dolls from scratch that looked like the queen
by the time the thread fell silent. Her hands are exactly like
mine—she could make anything. She was the first woman I
knew god in. She became my lighthouse.

*Granny used to tell me stories*

*She was six years old, in church that was held in a barn in the middle
of an old plantation in Louisiana. During the praise and worship she
was the only one who noticed the roof had caught fire. No one heard
her shouting, but when the roof began to collapse, the congregation
turned into a stampede and granny was trampled into the ground. She
was the last to make it out, but everyone survived.*

She told me this was the reason she didn't rush anymore
She never wanted to forget anything/
She didn't want anyone to feel forgotten

Not all forgotten things are godless things
         and she would not rush for godless things

She always rushed for me

Her light, a rapid staccato beacon to guide me home.


The second: Grandma. My mother's mother. Tall and
slender. All the white of a Canadian flag.
I have her nose and tongue. I do the best I can with the both of
them.
She'd sing, couldn't hold a single note, but she tried. She
danced. Motown. From something like 1960 to 2009 when her
legs no longer heard the music.
She'd say,
   *I used to be sweet on the military men back then, but your grandfather*
          *Sam-Cooke-crooned me down to America!*

She left a part of herself back home to love him. He did not
do the same in return, but this does not mean that he did not
fight. He beat her until color was no longer a line distinguishing
the two of them.

But he loved her.
Grandma was sick her entire life, but she was too much stubborn
to let the lupus stop her sassy. When I came out to her, she told
me I should go to San Francisco because *that's where we all live.*
I laughed, thanked her for pointing out the herd of fancy boys.

My grandmothers were the ones who cared the least about that sort of thing, and they were like sisters. They lived on the same street. Their bellies shook the same when they laughed at the banter.

Lighthouse and the boat I set sail on, into the cold wade that asks me politely to drown and they are the place I go to survive it. And to live it, and live, and live, and drift. Until I find my way home.

# seven layers of hell
*after Sierra DeMulder*

The first is fifty damp hands of people I do not know fondling my
ears

The second is a flood
of unidentified spiders
and I am trapped
in a short house of mirrors

The third is James Baldwin
reading poems on race and sexuality
while the KKK sings *America the Beautiful*
over him

The fourth is a photograph
of the boy who got away,
with his husband who looks somewhat like me,
and two laughing children
who do not

On the fifth
there are two chairs;
in one
sits my father's brother,
naked, erect, and drooling
in the other,
my last lover holding clenched fists strapped with brass knuckles;
both of them
staring
waiting for me to run

The sixth
is my mother and father
bound to two creaky rockers for the rest of their lives
to the first floor of my home;
as I nurse them daily,
they throw single dollar bills at my feet

And on the final floor,
the one that will certainly chain my wrists around the devil's
neck
the one that will burn me slowly from the shoulders down
is a hospital where my grandmothers spent their final day
their rooms are directly ahead of me,
                                    they are calling out my name
the elevator is made entirely of glass,
                          but the doors,

                    the doors


They do not open.

# recall, the first one

tear it open,
throw it
down
into the bag
or the bowl
hell,
the whole damn sink
if you like it
like that

do not be shy,
tear it open—
the flour,
shake it out
as much as you want to use
just make sure you use it

granny didn't like no soft chicken
she could use the most shallow of skillets,
but that oil,
it better be hot!

my small eyes
stretching over the sink to watch
but I bet'not tell the secrets!
and we never laughed smaller than a holler

the round surplus
of her hands moved
spice, and meat, and
white, and red around
the way articles are tossed when you tumble dry,
careless, but on purpose

this is the first love I learned:
all five senses keeping the thing I created

# resemblance, the first one

My father and my ex-lover are left/handed.

# grist of bees

My grandfather was a black leather recliner
every night he returned home from a 12-hour work shift

My nine cousins would fall at his feet
to greet him before scrambling away,

but I would settle into his lap
a brown-eyed, brown boy
laughing at the same television shows he did

My grandfather was a mechanic
and a charm of hummingbirds all at the same time

He was what it looked like
when love clocks in even after it clocks out.

My first great love
came as a grist of bees
a heavy hum
I only felt in my once winged
feet and tangled chest,

my chest has always been a honeycomb
it's sweet, but there are holes in it

Holes I tunneled into an exploration
of all the ways I care for myself
because you need holes to breathe,
and sometimes
I use holes
to tell stories,
to make love,
to bury what I know
to dig up what I don't

Like all the ways both
my father
        and first great love
could make a hive look like a clenched fist
and wring the honey out of me

The first time I saw
the furrow of their brows,
it was in their disapproval of
the other ones I loved

Asking to be loved by them
meant asking to be judged at the same time

The first time I felt
the tension in their wrists
was ten years old;
        the mallet of his fist lunged into the soft        soil of
my thigh —
last year
        when he choked another boy into a street

do you see how they are so close
they begin to sound like the same man?

When I finally heard
my father's voice escape
        my lover's mouth
it was the language —
        the fluency in *fuck you* —
familiar first,
then flinch,
stung me dry just the same

and then there are all the times
I have started over with the both of them:
a collapse of all the pretty parts
into a burning thing we thought we could hold on to
and it is breathtaking
— the birth of a star,

but what happens
when a star has nothing left to burn?

You get a quiet explosion,
        or a loud explosion,
or a violent explosion,
        or a black hole,
or a black leather recliner,
        somehow always ending in explosion

what a stellar nursery of men I have loved
in all my gravity and give

Then I remember that my grandfather was not my father's
blood,
my father's real father was a stone who only taught his seven
sons how to roll

My father is a heavy wheel spinning a groove in the road
and my ex-lover falls in line with this all too well

I have always been nothing more than a hive of black honey
who could love an old man home from work

Too thick for the hummingbirds to catch me,
but always right in line for the stone to strike

to break,
to form another hole
for the grist of bees to make a home out of

# i take after the women

There is a king-sized bed in the room we sleep in
It leaves too much space between us
I blame the bed
Not the person who bought it—
the man who reminds me of what he owns

I can no longer see the man I bend my light for
But I still blame the bed
Not the person lying in it
Not the person lying.

# resemblance, the second one

They were born in December,
not always a cold time though.

# mute

Dad can get real loud. Not always, but he sad. He always gets mad first though. I tried to tell him I know it hurts a lot. It's not that he wasn't listening, he just can't hear me over all the noise.

# recall, the second one

Daddy taught me how to tie my shoes.

the morning was a quiet study,
I only stood up to his knee

his face was the night's sky
and I was a stargazer
and it was he and I

it was never he and I

and we were in a rush
and I was falling behind
like children do

but he gave me time to learn these laces-

made a loop with each one, but
I always wrapped them twice
before pulling

that whole day
I tied and untied and tied again

this is the second way I learned to love:
to secure it all,                    tightly,          before letting it go.

# the night my father accompanies me to a gay bar

The air is a hot
Cast iron griddle
And everyone on the dance floor
Is a vessel of color and steam
Sizzling into
A pallet of sex
And dreaming boys

And my father is with me tonight
A very straight, black man
I never thought would say yes to me
who I said I wouldn't write poems about anymore

But ain't that what being a poet is?
Writing about the things we swear we're not gonna write about
anymore

Six months before this night,
My father almost killed himself
So he moved out
Admitted himself to some clinic
Where they don't let you visit
But you can drop off dirty laundry
And cigarettes

And I don't even smoke
But I inhaled two to the very end on my way to bring him things
he asked for

And do you know what it is to question
If whether this time will be the first time
You can save your father with a poisonous thing?

But this,
This poem is not about my father dying tonight
This poem is about the day my father decided to live, honey!

To be a redemption song for all we never had
Before now

I am too drunk to actually hear
The music that the DJ is playing
But I'm sure it is some Katy-Kesha-Britney mash up with Pitbull
rapping in the background because this is *still* North Carolina
and this is all they know
I am also too busy flirting with the boy my father met [and set me
up with] while he was in therapy
Because, of course, he thinks we date everyone,
But this one happens to be cute

Now my father ain't ever had no rhythm
But he continues to dance on the one and three beat anyway
His smile is the only song I need to hear

This time
he has set himself on fire
Not with the scorched tip of some rolled menthol and tobacco
But as the greatest act of love I have ever seen
So no, Paris is not burning tonight

We are merely two black boys still living in our bodies
Learning a new love for boys who have a love for boys who've
always been around
But we couldn't always see in our void
So we talk about it through our feet this time

Dancing in all this glitter
We notice how
the darkness
and our blackness are
not the same thing—
One says things are dim
Says *ain't no light around here boy*
Says you will certainly have trouble seeing

The other just wants to be alive
Says they just want to be seen
Says
Sometimes I strip down to my underwear
Before dancing in the dark
Light a few candles
in my living room
And pretend they are strobes
Popping off my body
Laughing at all the glow
some god don' stuffed me with

I know
It flickers sometimes

My father
He flickers sometimes too

# resemblance, the third one

Both of them have brothers. My father killed his. The truest
story was with granny, but she never told it. If she did, I don't
remember.

I watched him, as he threatened to kill *his* with a
screwdriver. The truest story is with the marks around my
neck. I tell it. I remember.

# when a boy tells you he loves you

it will be the first time you hear this
It is late, and
he isn't even there to tell you this in person,
but instead, from a car ride home from a bar in Chicago
He is there on business
and, of course, you will smile
because he sounds like he means it
because you believe him
because a boy has never handed those words to you
Like crushed blackberries in the palms of his hands
                                firm
                                young,
                                full,
                                    waiting to taste sweet with you

His arms creeping vines begging to touch the sun in your face
saying
*Here, take everything I have ever touched to be closer to you,*

His breath
waiting to be folded into a love note passed in between the nape
of your neck
and his front teeth;
He will remember the time you told him you felt safe in his
mouth,
he will never grow hungry,
just distant

When a boy tells you he loves you
You will hear music
The voice of your past lover dancing up your throat,
your stomach
an after-hours cabaret still waiting for the last call

That was when you learned that when a boy says,
*I love you,*
he means,
*I am getting ready to be inconsistent with you, now*

This boy will tell you that he loves you
not long after he had you waiting for two hours in front of a
cocktail lounge

Patience is something you were working on,
But no, not for him

When he asks you to tell him that you love him back,
it will be in a car
in the parking lot of a late night diner
You will watch the words fall into your lap like a spilled glass of
white wine
You will remember the day your courier pigeon heart got lost in
the wind
Because that was a message it did not know how or where to
carry

And one
        by one
                the boys have fallen as silent as the birds;

So eloquently they used to speak
until I asked the questions
that broke them into ghosts,
that bled me into a corpse with so many questions of my own for
the soil
but their tongues do not know simple

The things I should be hearing,
the things that will make us living men
in this time of insatiable, yet dying lovers

When a boy tells you he loves you for the first time
only to become silent like a folded sheet of tissue paper
not wanting you to decrease him into the truth
Do not crack your face into the fullest, crescent moon at the
tapered bottom of a blackened sky,
He never meant a single word of any of it

He is just a boy, remember?
Only another
sad,
silly boy,
remember?

# the beast takes its shape

The only time we use self defense is when we believe we are in
danger

My body is the meadow
He is the wind
So I am moving in every direction he throws me
and it is gentle
        at first.

I am always smiling myself into a lie

(I have a conversation with a friend about the man she's been
with—there are beasts everywhere; she believes to escape the
abuse would be to escape feeling comfortable; that she should
always want to fight back, but the only time we fight back is when
we know we are in danger—
        there are beasts everywhere)

        My lover tried to *kill* me once.
        I died everyday as practice,
        Let my green wilt
        Into a brittle of rust

        If he is the wind,
        then I am holding my breath,
        Waiting on the day I do not allow my lungs to turn from
        me

        Months ago, I attempted to leave
        *If we believe in us*
        *we must be two people who refuse to give up on each other,*
        He cried,
        Asked me to stay
        Made a false love to me where I stood

When it wants something,
A beast will show you how human it can act,
Will shift the growl into a moan
Will sink his teeth into your neck and call it a kiss

The only time we use self defense is when we believe we
are in danger
If I let him inside of me, was I still in danger?

You do not need danger to save your own life, only fear
Only all the thoughts rushing out of you as the home you
raised them in grows dark

Did I not fear my father enough to stop me from loving a
man into his silhouette?
Do I think I can love a monster back into a man?
Do I believe love means growing so afraid of a man that I
never give myself permission to leave?

I am just the meadow,
A flat plain to which all his kite-string
Run
And
Unravel
Can stomp a boy's boot into

I believe I am loving him back into a boy again
Who laughs with a howling wind behind him

I want him to open his fists

I am an open field,
The beast does not rest in me

I will not defend myself
I will not love you into a dangerous place

Oh god
You are everywhere,
Open your fists
Please

Just open your fists

# sometimes

Sometimes
I am driving
And thinking
About how unhappy I was
And how much rage
I filled you with
And what a grand nod
To my own power
To be able to do that,
To fill a man with so much


Imagine
What all that
Full would've done
If it were love there
Instead?

# the truth

is
I was never the one
He was never the one.

Every day is a finger
my hands no longer need
      A rake I send away
      to return shovel
      for the dig

Each one a stem
I pluck from a garden
that never grew here,

but I do not pity the dead
I do not look for the boy
who does not know
what he wants
Who does not care
to look where he is throwing
the stone
just because
there is a dark well before him

Boys do that, you know?
Wish for a place
with no idea where to go

Go to the one
who will love you with familiar

To the one who loved another, too

I could no longer be with the one
who does not know what they are doing

That is your good grace,
that is okay for you,
but I am moving on now
giving what I have left:
my open mouth
        my want
these eyes
        lethal onyx stones
my inner thigh
        your favorite part that no longer
        belongs to you because I say so
my dockside wait
my quiet honey
my runaway song
my shuttering window
my laughing shotgun
my praying, midnight swaddle
my ticking clock of please
my cemetery of listen
        the place where all things
        I have heard go
        to die because
        I only love into living
My painted revival
        and how I always handed it all back
        How I never asked for anything back

How I just want to be loved, but do not ask to be filled up

Meaning love is a bucket of water
        evaporating over hot coals,
a verb
        for all of the things we can carry
        while it is burning,
my love is just a word
        I use for holding more burning things than I can carry,


Because love explains all
of the things that are not possible

like my thank you,
        my gracious smile,
My thank you,
        my bent knees,
My thank you,
        my wake up today,

My begging you not to beg me to stay

My stay,
>how I wanted everything to be so different;

My stay,

My stay,
>and the last time should have been the last time,

My goodbye,
>but it will be this time.

My leave,

My now.

>I hope he is a good fuck, I really do.
>I hope he makes you forget everything.
>This time.

My first hello.

# always a hotel somewhere

That armchair in the corner
of a hotel room that watches you sleep;

it's what I saw as I packed
my bag this morning


Years ago,
there was a burgundy one quite like it
In a room we checked into
on some holiday, I imagine, when you cared most maybe,


or
this was the room booked after that concert
you took me to, but planned for another man to come
In case I wouldn't show

regardless,
my body still rode yours
in the armchair beneath us

We were burgundy floating at midnight,


before the blood

# recall, the third one

the number two toe
at the head
of the knuckle
of my second metatarsal
on my right foot
is broken

I don't remember when this happened exactly [during the fight];

I know that I am still living enough
to be angry
every time I look at it now.

# on love

It is a fist
It is the body attached

When it begs you,
Do not be the answer

Why would I stay
to silence my footsteps?
to scratch the walls of a howling lavender?

You cannot feast on an empty house.

To love a man is to say:
It is not.
Unless he is stealing you from across a table, and

you watch
each
piece
leaving
on a spread that you designed

# i, ghost,

a lonely chiffon flag
a morsel of cloud
on a night
ravenous
for my raw threads

I am my own haunt

# some nights

I call a man over to fuck,
and then we do.

Other nights
He will lie in my bed,
his body a cavern of
wet     grinning teeth
mine, a canyon unwound
Observing everything I can see
with the lights off;

in my smallest voice
I tell him to leave,
before he has traveled me,

Of course,
he is a confused, but
silent child
wandering into the dark
asking me to find him again.

I lock the door behind him,
stretch myself down,
and masturbate to vintage porn
and the thought of a past lover
with one of his past lovers

I ask myself,

Is this not what it means to be in love with me?

# an observation

I have seen a lot of penises
In my life
And they are really
Quite disgusting creatures

Ones that turn
Downward
Eager to dive into you

Ones that go left
Or
Right
Not knowing where they are going
Telling you
The man they are attached to
Is such a lost boy

Ones that curl upward
A snobbish tail
Who believes he is bigger
Than he really is

The things an ego does to a man

Fat squishy ones
That flop at your touch
Stiffen
Softly
I really just want to hold it
Where will you put it all?

The skinny ones
[I almost dare not say]
A sharp tongue
Taking up space
But not filling it with much

The micros
you know, the very small ones
Of course
I would not forget
Your hidden language
Telling a body to
focus on the rest of the body

Then there are the straight ones
The ones with clear direction
The ones that know exactly
Where they want to go
Those are the most terrifying
Of them all

They go deeper
And harder
And faster
They do not listen
No matter how painful
You tell them it is

# three weeks

*There is a feature in my phone that keeps track of all of the locations I frequent. After it records my location enough times, it begins identifying what those places are and the times that I am usually there.*

About a month ago, my ex-boyfriend tries to kill me.
His hands
a serpent's grip
Full of coil and bite
and my neck,
a nocturnal mouse
wondering where I got all this safe from to think I could run
when I wanted

I do not fight back
by choice.

I do not wish for yesterday's
smoking furnace
A kiss of heat that would burn
just as quick as it would blow up when I wasn't looking

Normally,
I'm always looking.

I flee with not nearly all of my belongings;
Three weeks
without the things that belong to me
In a new place,
And the feature in my phone keeps telling me I have to go back
Tells me I'm not finished
Thinks I should smell the carmine air that still crawls beneath
my skin
And in my sheets
And on my bare feet.

The court grants me the right to everything mine.
I collect them as cold, grainy stones
in the bottom of a river I once called love.

There's a feature in my phone that still records the places I
frequent most and labels them accordingly

For three weeks
my new address is just that:
New

And after three weeks,
after all my stuff—
The feature in my phone—
It tells me I am home.

It tells me
I am home.

# the opening

I opened his *no* and out fell a closet
I opened his closet and out fell a handful of tiny swords
I opened the swords and inside was a cave of glitter

I opened the cave of glitter and inside was an altar
I opened the altar and out fell a crying boy
I opened the crying boy and inside was a desert

I opened the desert and inside, a stretch of copper wire from his
chest to my chest
I opened the wire and out fell the tears
I opened the tears and inside were two small hands
I opened the hands and inside were smaller children

I opened the children and inside was laughter
I opened the laughter and out fell a set of scales
I opened the scales and inside were eyes
I opened the eyes and inside was air
I opened the air and out fell a fetch of dragonflies

I opened the dragonflies and inside was an anchor
I opened the anchor and out fell a meadow
I opened the meadow and inside was a fence of swinging chains

I opened the fence and out fell a bottomless pool
I opened the pool and inside was my *yes*
I opened my *yes* and inside was my wait
I opened my wait and out fell a rusty chair

I opened the chair and inside, a rocking heart.

# first response to my father's message

It is morning—

Not
My morning

The grey has had time to nest

Grabbed every edge of light,

Every twig and stone

Found

In you.

Time is moving, and
going nowhere

My father has found his voice again
I don't know where he is,
But it has found me

It is a practiced crawl
And I am a mother encouraging her old young home
Never a child stretching my limbs out from its mouth

I cannot bend the teeth behind me
The bones:
The ones I drag

The ones that vaguely carry his body

cannot be respelled

Today,
the men don't stop smilin', but
I don't trust 'em

I have seen the things their teeth spell out—

I loved once.

If I remember my father,

never leaving home,

I'd become the salt beneath his collar
His cigarette hovering above my head
Subtracting his body to save me under his breath;

I would let him stay here, today

where a man asks me to come smile with him;

I do not.

I used to be the kind of man who would wait on a man

And now—

# Acknowledgments

To Los Angeles, my city, the great basin of smog that offered the friends I choose as family. Joslyn, Vanessa, Joel, Bird, Vee, Carolyn, Fisseha, Donny, Venessa, Ashley, Jasmine, Shihan, Javon, Katrina, Yesika, Angie, Lindsay, Ethan, Danielle, Jason, and Can'Dase. Thank you, thank you.

To Shaun, Mama Sandra, Aunt Norma, Jennifer, and Chris, it was so critical for you all to be where you were at that point in my life. Thank you for keeping me close.

To my children all over this city. Chestina, Sheila, Lauren, Stephanie, and Kevin, I am so grateful and so proud of you.

To NOT A CULT for listening, and believing in the small, queer, black boy and his queer black words when you could've chosen anyone else in the world.

To the Los Angeles LGBT Center for hearing me when the police department wouldn't, when my body would not stop proofreading the night, and when I had to walk into a courtroom to defend myself—a free attorney at my side.

My father, for not giving up on yourself when you said so many times that you would.

To the lover who will one day find me, here, look at all that I have unfurled. For you. For us to finally rest.

If you or someone you know is in an abusive relationship and in need of immediate help, please use any of these resources:

**The Los Angeles LGBT Center**
1220 N. Highland Avenue
Los Angeles, CA 90038
(323) 860-2280

**The National Domestic Violence Hotline**
1-800-799-7233

**Peace Over Violence**
1015 Wilshire Boulevard, Suite 200
Los Angeles, CA 90017
(213) 955-9090
24 hr hotline: (310) 392-8381

Please seek help as soon as possible. You do not deserve to be abused by anyone. You are so loved. You are always enough. Always.

# About the Author

**Edwin Bodney** is a nationally recognized poet, performer, and educator born and raised in Los Angeles. Throughout his career, he has had the privilege of working with creative writing students of all ages, most notably at California School of the Arts, as well as sharing his work with organizations like: USC, UCLA, Lexus, FourTwoNine Magazine, and Platypus Press.

One of his finest accomplishments is having *A Study of Hands* incorporated into the creative writing program at the University of Wisconsin-Madison.

Bodney currently resides in Los Angeles, and can be found hosting Da Poetry Lounge on Tuesday nights or eating carbs with his cat.